AF413286

# Between The Lines

## Ramyiah LaShay Faison

# Table of contents

## Dedication

This book is dedicated to my angelic grandmother, Billie Jean, who Allah confirmed the writing of this book through. Thank you for believing in me, grandma. To my big brother, Ronald, who is now in the spiritual realm. Every experience I have, he is a part of. To my mother who has taught me resilience and strength. To my father who has nurtured my creativity.

Thank you.

# Introduction

"Between The Lines" is not only a poetic book, but it is full of wisdom from my heart to yours. Since a child, I always knew I was a writer. I would write letters to my grandmother, expressing my feelings about something she did that I liked or disliked. I stayed up past my bedtime, typing poems into my notes app. Journaling was the way I coped with the difficulties and excitements of life. It allowed me to create a sacred space for deep connection with myself and gain an abundance of self-awareness at a very young age. Without the presence of writing in my life, I wouldn't be who I am today. As a little girl, I knew that one day I would be the author of a book that would be a gift to the world. It would talk about the "in-betweens" of life— you know, those moments that carry us from one point to another, those moments that are often disregarded. In this world, people often converse about the "black-and-white" aspects of life, but the "gray" areas are often neglected, glossed over, and left out. Do we ever take time to speak them aloud, reflect on them, write them down, embrace them, or even acknowledge them?

In this book, you will be taken through the divine journey of these moments in my life. Chapter 1 is called *The Unlearning*, and Chapter 2 is called *The Rebirth*. In the cycles of life, we are always unlearning, relearning, and being made new, over and over again. You may find that you relate to these thoughts and feelings in your own way, for our experiences are unique. Still, I encourage you to allow yourself to reflect. Each page you read is an opportunity for you to reflect on some of the special moments that brought you to each milestone in your life. My prayer is that you feel heard, seen, and validated, as I have allowed myself to feel heard, seen, and validated (by Allah and myself). May this book be one of wisdom, love, and understanding for all who find it in their hearts to read it.

# Chapter 1: The Unlearning

You've died so many times to fit into what you thought was the thing to be & every time you've died, the god in you has suffered the immense, smothering pain of self-neglect and self-rejection. Tell me, when did you first entertain the belief that a box is your place to be? forcing yourself into rigid parameters that your soul had already outgrown the very moment you even considered limiting your divine potential. How could you fit into an enclosed space created by man of this world when you are a direct reflection and descendant of Allah (God) Himself? If we fed more on the knowledge of God, we would understand and therefore nurture ourselves on a higher level.

— we are universal beings made from triple darkness.

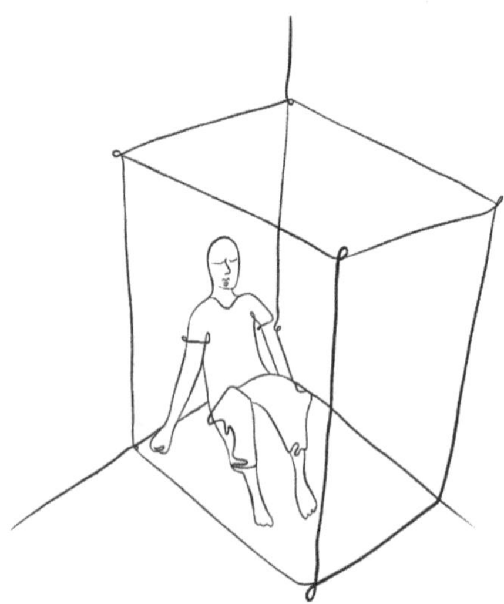

I think to myself, how do I trust what feels like love to me in this stage of healing?

Do I just hope for the best?

What feels like love to me may be the very opposite of the love Allah desires for me.

Start where you are, but don't stay there.

– stepping stones

He asked me, "Do you know how to live in real life?"

Do I?

— social media is a world, too.

How can we get deep in the mud with our people to save them, when we refuse to get deep in the mud with ourselves?

–it starts with ourselves.

Laziness and idleness reek the staleness of untouched potential.

What manner of woman is this, that she would keep walking under heavy trial?

Heels bruised, but still stepping.

Eyes tired, but still glistening.

Carrying pain, but still healing.

If every unreleased tear fell, an ocean would emerge.

What manner of woman is this?

A woman who found God.

A woman who is being repaired by her Creator, as only He can do for her.

A woman who surrendered fully to God, giving the Best Knower all of her pain, her worries, her stress.

A woman who maketh her God sufficient for the rest of her days.

A woman with expectations of God and not man.

– a godly woman

Move through the canal of familiarity and walk through the fire of refinement, that Allah may strip you of what cannot come with you.

-trials purify 333

I love being a light to others.

Allah has put a natural desire in me to help others, and when I allow my ego to control my approach, I find that there's very little nourishment in return, and very little nourishment for those Allah could've touched through me with His perfect love.

To do things for self-exaltation and self-indulgence is a waste of time, and I despise wasting time.

 I strive to keep vanity out of the work Allah puts on my heart to do by wanting more for myself and humanity through my love for the Creator Himself."

— "How do you keep self-indulgence and vanity out of your actions?"

Black woman.

Her movement exudes poetry and soul

Walking to the rhythm of the cosmos, heaven running through her veins so sweetly.

9 ether hair covered with silk and satin fabrics, woven by her own hands on her countryside land

Black nose pointed to the heavens, watching for the wheels.

She has expectations of Him.

Feet planted so heavily into the Earth,

She is Allah's mercy personified.

She dances for the glory of her Creator, for He Allah (God), is the only reality.

Dance is her communication to Allah, her reverence to Allah.

This feels like home.

−Second self of Allah

Spend time feeding your good habits.

Spend no time feeding your bad ones. Allow them to starve.

-focus your intention.

The answer to your prayers is found in helping yourself and striving to be a better *you*.

God helps those who help themselves. Give yourself a helping hand.

– Be your own rock first.

Prayer doesn't stop at talking to the Creator. Prayer is also in the work that we do to have our prayers answered.

– no mystery God

Mirrors.

Allah (God) is looking at Himself when we look at each other.

He is the only reality.

How beautiful it is that Allah is speaking through you and back to Himself.

- Peace be unto you.

Whatever truth I know, it is my duty (if Allah pleases) to share that truth for the good of myself and the good of people. Share with others the same truth that saved you.

– Islam saved my life.

And when you get to where you're going so fast, you realize the painful yet beautiful truth: it was never all about the destination.

That's your thing, not His thing.

That's your compartmentalized thinking, not His infinite thinking.

A perfect example of making it all about the destination is seen in the hustle culture of today..

chronic, relentless desire to achieve but not to breathe?

not to rest?

not to stop and thank the Lord for what is now and what is to come next?

Unfriendly to reflection and gratitude. That's what hustle culture is.

It was never about the destination.

Do you believe you were put here to just run past a finish line?

Take a look at the journey, love.

Look at all of the mileage you've attempted to skip over by walking from the start line across the field to the finish line
And now, you have nothing to show for it because you didn't experience joy,

and you didn't experience joy because you didn't experience pain,

and you didn't experience pain because you backed out of the race of life and took the shortcut –
and that shortcut you took also cut your life force short without you knowing it.

Ah, but now you see that it's about who you are becoming on the journey to your destination. *Becoming.*

There's a sweet undertone about being intentional in your overall existence.

 Something so sweet about moving with purpose, ascending into the one who Allah knew you could always be.

That one you keep thinking of.

That one you find yourself experiencing glimpses of.

That one to whom all of your desired blessings are attached.

You'll reach that destination, but until then...

You are living in the journey. Don't pass through it without acknowledgment and gratitude.

Don't you walk across this field.

Rise to the challenge and run your race.

—And she found that when she reached the destination, it was all about the sojourn, the transformation.

The most difficult yet freeing study that I've ever pursued is the study of self.

–knowledge of self

When you love yourself as yourself, you desire that which loves you as yourself, too.

—just as Allah does

You have to see it in you first.

Waste no time waiting for others to see it in you.

 It starts with you.

 It starts with you.

It starts with you.

There has never been one like you, and after you, there will never be another like you.

You are a unique expression of the Creator.

– walk like you know that.

Don't look at trials as circumstances coming to mess up your *perfect* life.

 Look at trials as tests of faith that come to perfect you as a human being.

—motion

Allah made us in pairs.

Weathering storms is easier when you are here.

He is my maintainer, my provider, my protector, my rock, in this dimension and the next.

I love you, black man.

— The Black man is God.

For so long, I've waited for myself to be ready, to believe in me, to see my efforts through, until I realized that belief in myself alone was never meant to be enough. We were never meant to be vessels without an All-Knowing, All-Encompassing God Who guideth the feet of those whom He pleases to guide. We were never meant to be vessels without the Source of all life, intervening on our behalf. We were never meant to be independent of the One Who's help we all depend on for our sustenance, our life. So no, I'm not enough all on my own, and that's perfect for Allah. What need would I have of Him if I could suffice all of my own needs, guideth my own feet, straighten my own crooked path? Hm. Seek His face in all things...and even the times you've turned back to rely on yourself, taking matters into your own hands, He has exhausted all of your resources that you may come back to Him, over and over again, out of His mercy for your own good.

-note to self

I met comparison at a very young age, always having her hand over my mouth and doing her best to extinguish the flickering flame inside.

She doesn't want me to be great, and the moment I am blessed with a glimpse of who Allah has made me to be, she comes back, stomping, to put me under the cover of darkness and despair. Sometimes, she'll creep up on me without making a sound.

Other times, I hear the floorboards of my mind creek before she can get to me. We fought day in and day out... I fought my hardest, my strongest, my best.

She fought her hardest, her strongest, her best.

It wasn't until I sought refuge in Allah that I was able to fight her off and get a breather, but only for a time.

She has made a nuisance of herself in my home. She cannot live here.

- struggle is ordained.

You're so focused on the destination that you cannot see the present time as a present for yourself.
You're walking with closed eyes in a field of things that were meant to prepare you for
where you're going.
Your trials walk towards you, but you have your eyes closed, so you're presented with more and
more until the choice to close your eyes is removed from your control.
Your blessings whisper sweetly to you, but you have your ears closed and so you don't hear them
beckoning you to come closer.
Your lessons take you by your hand, but you have your heart closed and so you pull away
because you *don't have time* to be present right now.
When will you have time?

What's more important than the now?

Have you considered that the *now* is trying to teach you something?

– give yourself permission to be present.

The more I focus my energy on justifying my existence in this life that Allah gave to me, the closer I get to discovering my purpose.

The closer I get to discovering my purpose, the closer I become to fulfilling my purpose.

The closer I become to fulfilling my purpose, the more of that which Allah doesn't want for me is made clearer to me – causing that which is not for me to fall away from what I desire and that which is for me is also made clearer to me, moving towards me in a beautiful manner.

With Allah, peace is always around the corner or already here to bask in.


— Allah is sufficient for me.

How can you...feel comfortable *all* of the time– *and* –go through the fire of refinement? Sometimes, you're so focused on feeling good that you miss the glory, the lesson, the message.. attached to the circumstance.

Turn to Allah for all of your worries. He is the first and only line of refuge.

– take it to Him first; there is no God besides Him

A heart fervent for His love.

A spirit fervent for His presence.

A body fervent for His choice of residence.

—thirsting after righteousness

What if your greatest fear is your greatest gift?

What if that is the very thing you need to do in order to liberate yourself and your people?

What if running from the encounter with that fear is the very thing that keeps you imprisoned?

What if dealing with that fear is the very thing that will cause you to rise up out of the condition you are in?

— curiosities of a courageous mind

The type to keep the desires of her heart between her and God.

Why does it anger others, when I am not willing to share something so intimate?

What obligation does anyone have to announce the plans for their life?

Do those asking, have their lives all figured out?

I may know where I'm going, or I may not know... but who's asking, and why are they upset?

 The feet of the vessel can be moving, but what soul can see the remainder of their journey in its entirety?

Only Allah knows, and though I don't know all that is to come, there's something about it that feels so right,

down to the heavenly core of my being.

Headed in a direction my eyes haven't seen and ears haven't heard...

but with a willing heart, I walk with Him.

That's called *faith*.

Imagine if we knew it all.

What need would we have for prayer,

fasting,

studying the word,

And cultivating a strong relationship with Allah (God)?

What need would we have for life, when life is all about learning?

I breathe deeply as I affirm this truth: "I let go of the notion that I must have it all figured out right

now." Trusting God has looked like having flour, eggs, butter, sugar, and icing but not knowing how they all relate to make a cake.
No, not everything makes sense right now, but a recipe is forthcoming.

As we move our feet in obedience, here comes the understanding.

"What is the *now* trying to teach me?"

So..

If I don't announce my goals to her, him, or anyone else, that's okay.

I am not obligated to share the desires of my heart with anyone outside of myself and Allah.

I won't answer to anyone but Him when my time runs out, and there will be no one else to answer to when I am asked the big question: "What did you do with the time I gave you?"
I'd rather get busy doing the work and allow the desires of my heart and what He has in store for me to be *seen.*
I prefer that it become flesh, first.

Then, you will receive the answer to your question.

-unconventional thinking

He is after your heart.

There's freedom in being *real* in your walk with God,

real as in accepting who you are, where you are, and what *is* right now.

Real as in embracing the genuine, organic relationship you have with Allah, the same divine relationship you

keep running away from because it doesn't look like everyone else's relationship with Him...

Not understanding that every relationship with Allah is unique, considering who we are, our different experiences, and our different life missions.
If we aren't real with ourselves and God, where does He have room to intervene, to mold us into who He has called us to be?

Sure, you can look the part, but looking the part and being the part are two different things.

Sure, you can act the part, but there's performance and then there's the condition of the heart.

The condition of the heart impacts the quality of the performance.

What's the condition of your heart?

How does this condition express itself in your performance?

Are you truly well?

— self analysis

I am no longer an outlet that people can plug themselves into when they are running low on energy.

That's what being a giver without boundaries can do to you.

A giver without knowledge of my capacity to give without emptying my entire cup.

What did I have left for myself?

If I spend all of my time being dutiful to others, when do I find time to be dutiful to me?

How can I love myself without being dutiful to myself?

and in the same vein, how could I truly love others when I am struggling to love myself?

Understand that **when** you delay YOU when you need yourself most ,

**then** self- love quivers under the shadow of neglect,

ceasing to exist due to being choked out by the entertainment of things that were *more important*

than cultivating a genuine , deep relationship with self

and God.

— love is duty

interlude


Unlearning and Relearning the meaning of beauty.

Unlearning and Relearning the meaning of worthiness.

Unlearning and Relearning what it means to be spiritual.

Unlearning and Relearning the notion of strength.

Unlearning and Relearning the meaning of love.

Unlearning and relearning my position on Mother Earth in the Kingdom of God.

-undoing and rebuilding with knowledge of who I am in His eyes

# Chapter 2: The Rebirth

There's someone for everyone in this world. You will know you've found that someone when your soul releases a deep exhale, finally laying back onto the inner walls of your vessel with ease and relaxation. You will know when you've found that one for you when your intuition says that you won't have to spend a lifetime translating your soul, your essence.

They . Just . Get . You .

You won't have to crush yourself into boxes that you were never created to be in, cover your light with the blanket of fear, extinguish your fiery heart so full of passion with the strong breath of "I don't get you."

But consider this. Have you received yourself first?

-to be received is to receive yourself first.

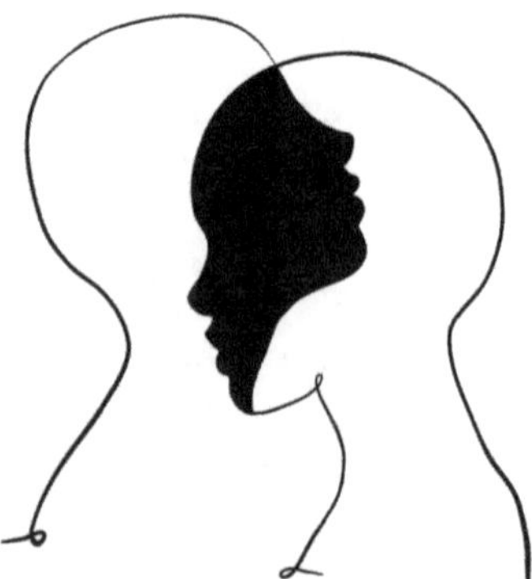

He wants you as you are *right now.* He can take you and make you new, but you have to come as a child... But if you're "too grown for this," then *this* may not sit right with you.

He doesn't want only the best parts of you, the parts that you constantly put on display, the parts of you that everyone loves. He wants the whole you, in your entirety.
He targets your weakest areas so that you may become stronger.

There's life in *motion*, and who you are in this moment is only for a time, because Allah will not allow you to stand in this phase for too long.
You'll witness this truth during stagnancy and feel the shaking of the ground beneath your feet to keep you moving toward Him.
In all of His doings, there is mercy.

He loves you as you are but you cannot stay as you are, where you are.

So, come get your healing; He wants to nourish the *whole* of you.

There is nowhere to run but to Him.

– no greater love

Bet on yourself.

Bet on not only your ability to share knowledge

 but also the effectiveness of the delivery of the knowledge you are sharing.

Come out of ignorance, and come into knowing.

– everything you need is already inside, butterfly.

Once life becomes good and "too good to be true"..

Instead of sabotaging it, embrace it..

*lean* into it..

 trust it with all of your heart.

Allah's mercy and grace are ever-present.

– reassurance

I hear colors. I smell colors. I feel in colors. I experience in color. I often question why Allah gave

me this gift. Why do I receive my environment this way? What
am I to do with this?

It's somewhere between expressing a message through visualization of color in my mind and exuding the colors, allowing them to be reflected in the work He has called me to do on this Earth.

When I speak certain words, hear certain things, smell certain aromas, colors interact with my soul.

When I hear the name "Khadijah," I hear pink.

Oftentimes, names with a strong "J" sound so blue to me.

When I hear bass sounding in a song, I feel and smell a cobalt blue blended with a deep purple.

When I smell frankincense and myrrh, I taste hues of orange and brown on a spiritual note.

Soulful harmonies stir up an elixir of magenta and royal blue.

Colors speak to the human experience.

It is therapy + life embodied.

With this spiritual sensory,

I shall *breathe* life into my life's purpose,

as Allah *breathed* life into each of us.

– Gifted

I want to be like Jesus.

I am always listening for a *sound* from my Lord.

The type of girl to say out of my mouth what others are afraid to think.

I know who backs me so fear is choked out by repeated affirmations of what HE said about me.

Bravehearted.

Soulful.

Sweet.

Dainty but Deadly.

I am protected by angels and ancestors.

Above all, I am protected by Allah.

My feet move at the rhythm of divine cadence.

When the Lord calls a cadence and then says "move," I *MOVE*

. And I move with strength, laser-focus, courage, endurance, deep-rooted faith, a pure heart...

and on my face, you can see that I didn't come to play.

— the heart of a believer

Why settle for drought when you can have abundance?

Settle for breadcrumbs when you can have the entire loaf

Settle for coals when you can have diamonds

Settle for faint love that feels like pulling teeth, when you can have true love that enters the room before you lift your finger to request it ... a love you would expect at 4:45 but greeted you by 4:44.

The kind of love that fills every corner of the room.

Real love.

The love that provides so much room for you to love with every fiber of your being, without the thought of having to tame it..

settle for "almost" when you can have *exactly* what your heart desires..

Almost was never enough, and you *know* this.

— Seek Allah first.

Embracing the fire taught me how to keep my sanity.

I prayed for divine guidance and Allah presented me with an opportunity to be guided.

– it's up to me to take it.

True success is enjoying your own company.

True success is finding solace in sitting with yourself with no need to engage in escapism.

True success is freedom of expression, of mind, heart, and soul.

True success is in liberation of self and the people.

True success is depending on Allah to get you through everything by opening up your mouth and talking with Him.

True success is doing what you love.

— what does true success mean to you?

Movement is sacred.
Dance is sacred.
Where there's life, there's motion..
and where there's stagnancy, there's death.
Movement conveys a message, expresses an idea.
Movement is information, just as our DNA is information.
It is a way of communicating emotions when words don't suffice.
Dance is a storehouse of complete restoration.
Down the wheel of time, our avenue through which we've released suppressed emotions, stagnant energy, toxins from our bodies, and troubled thoughts.
What do you think Black ancestors were doing amid troubled times?
Dance nourishes my body, mind, and soul It enriches my experience, as well as my perspective, no matter the circumstances.
When I dance, I know I am directly communicating with Allah.
I feel my senses heighten.
I feel chills in my body.
I see myself in a beautiful light because I'm seeing His light radiate through me.
Every step is a form of prayer in gratitude to God for blessing me with this gift.
My dance is not just me moving, It is me accessing higher forms of consciousness in ways I cannot explain.
When I dance, I am creating a sanctuary of my own to praise Allah.
I am in tune with my angels, my ancestors, Allah Himself, and the cosmos.
I feel alive.
Dance will always be a part of me; it is one of many gifts Allah would never let me get too far from.
– a dancer in Islam

The physical part of dance that we see with our two eyes is just the tip of the iceberg.

There's a spiritual component, a transcendental experience that is rooted deeply in nobody but the Creator of the Heavens and the Earth.
A pointed foot likened unto a paintbrush to a canvas, painting flying colors across the atmosphere reaching for the heavens.
Telling untold stories with the eyes.

A gentle, sweet wind caresses the face while ascending to higher dimensions.

Vessel taken over by the source of strength.

Mind at ease, but the body is in motion.

This is pure meditation.

This is Allah speaking back to Himself through His creation.

Blessed is the creation that has the opportunity to sit in on this conversation.

You have that opportunity, if you allow yourself to have it.

– anchor yourself in Him.

Ringing ears.

Angel numbers.

Astral projection.

Nature's Frequency.

Prayer.

Warm winds.

Food from the Earth.

Wisdom from grandma's porch.

Sure of yourself.

Clean water.

Light-footed men and women.

Heightened senses.

Orbs in sight.

Brown hands adorned with gold.

Divine auras everywhere.

Attracting butterflies.

Angels moving on your behalf.

Herbalists.

Sages.

Medicine men and women.

Sustainable living.

— Blessings from Allah

No matter what trial befalls you, always keep your heart soft, open, and pliable for your Creator.

– a heart of flesh

Keeping my head in a book, flowers in my reach, my body clothed in dignity, and my existence covered in prayer has saved me from much heartbreak.
Islam is peace.
– it is a way of life

Desiring always to be meditating and reflecting on the Originator of the heavens and the earth

Yearning for my thoughts and actions to revolve around Him, like the 9 planets that revolve around the Sun.
Stronger than a covalent bond.

Desiring nothing to come between us.

A bond so strong that not an atom on the planet Earth could sever us.

—We are One for Eternity

When you are flying high, some turbulence is guaranteed.

— but we still go high

Dare to be yourself and see who remains. They are for you, truly.

Dare to be yourself and see what remains. These are for you, truly.

— what's for you is for you, trust that.

I've had to lay past versions of myself to rest so many times.

Something about seeing the old me lying there with an inviting smile, made it hard for me

to let go.

She, her, and her — they were all that I knew.

She smiled that inviting smile.

She smiled that "come back to me" smile.

 That's how she got me the last time, but this time will be different.

There is no weed here to choke out the life of the seed of truth taking root in me.

The clock strikes 5:55 a divine reminder that justice is being served for all of the suffering

I've endured to exist vertically (upright)

as my former selves lay there horizontally.

I love them dearly, but I love who I am becoming in His name, more.

– the revival

How could someone be more beautiful than me and they are not like me?

 How could I be more beautiful than someone else and I am not like them?

How can we deem one thing as "more than" or "less than" the other, when they are not alike?

How can we compare two things that aren't alike?

Perhaps, *more* and *less* are subjective.

 –Beauty is in the eye of the beholder

Stillness is a quick way to figure out who you are.

When we are still, we truly have nothing to distract ourselves from whatever thoughts or feelings that may arise within us.

In stillness, this is where we really find out who we are, why we are here, and how we are truly feeling.

Stillness forces us to face what we've been suppressing or holding in.

Stillness can be very painful and difficult for people, especially living in a world full of distractions from what is really here on Earth.

When we choose to be still, we lift the veil from upon our eyes.

   - 2021 college journal entry

Building generational wealth by how you take care of your well-being is so important.
- 2021 college journal entry

Something about those southern trees that draws my focus in like a big hug from grandma.

They're full of wisdom...They've seen so much.

At the touch of the trunk, I serve as a medium between the physical realm and spiritual realm.

The fresh air blew in my reddish-brown tresses and made itself at home in my lungs.

Sitting pretty near the bayou, reminiscing on what was and what is.

When I see the ocean, I don't just see a body of water.

I see the water that held the bodies of my ancestors, the water that carried boatloads of unwilling bodies across it.

Hm,

The aroma of rainfall greets me with its warm embrace as I sit on my porch, in my rocking chair.

Harvesting herbs, vegetables, fruits, and grains from land I proudly call my own.

Soil rich with fertility and nutrients.

Unusual girl, time travel is how she copes at times.

That puzzle piece that doesn't quite fit the structure.

Wise beyond her years.

The sweet company of elders feels like home to her soul

Déjà vu, it's nothing new.

Hat tilted to the side and brown eyes, lookin' just like her daddy.

Village girl, with a heart yearning for that southern living since a baby.

The desire to live simply, void of the spirit of vanity.

Record players, candles, woven baskets, satin gowns

Old soul, young soul, existing simultaneously within her.

Creole Belle, Indigenous woman.

Olga's Great-Grandchild.

–Southern Soul

"Put away your worries for now. It can wait."

It doesn't sit right with me to "put away" my worry "for now."

I want it to leave *now.*

I do not desire to see it when I return from whatever it is I am doing to help me cope with this worry.
If I must worry after this, I would rather it be a worry of something else.

Not the same worry that I "put away" for the moment.

But then again,

Maybe that worry needs to be put aside so that we clear the way for deep healing, even if it's just for a time.
To heal the *root* of the issue, recognize that the worry you feel is the product, the fruit of your foundation.
It takes grace, introspection, and quietness of mind.

It can take losing your mind just to find your peace of mind.

When we choose to engage in the act of healing,

We also choose the peace that comes with chaos,

The difficulty that comes with ease

The climax and the valley.

— struggles of the mind and heart

And in that moment, she realized that things won't change unless her mind does...

What is this chaos that I feel so deep in my soul?

Why does it seem so hard to feel less empty and feel more whole, more often?

Life is catching up to me as I make a sharp left, trying to run from my problems and the broken promises unkept .. to myself.

19 is an age of realization for me, and this is not just any kind of awakening.

 It's the kind of awakening that makes you want to scream, making the entire Earth shake.

It's the kind of awakening that has you annoyed with everyone around you because you are going through your own obstacles.
It is the kind of awakening that causes you to notice synchronicity throughout the week as a reminder that you are divinely protected and guided.
It is the kind of awakening that makes you want to end all of this and get away from everyone and everything.
Frustration precedes change.

— the age of rebirth

Learning that I am the woman of God, that my sisters are the women of God, has changed my life and my perspective of who I am completely. Being *told* that I am something is one thing. People have *told* me all my life that I am beautiful, sunny, sweet, whatever compliment it may be .. but I've always wondered what I was beyond that.. because although those things are wonderful qualities to have, they are incomparable to the *intrinsic value* and *nature* of a woman of God. It's already in our nature before anyone offers their perception of us .. and it is still there during and after that perception is given to us. I am thankful for the spiritual teacher in my life, for teaching me my value as a woman of Allah and for giving me the actual meaning of what that is. Not only has he given meaning to it, but he also has taught me how to conduct myself as the second self of God. It's one thing to know *what* I am, but knowing *how* to carry myself as such a serious act of creation makes it long- lasting and solid.
— I thank Allah for the teachings.

It isn't difficult, it is clear to see, that there is only one Ramyiah and only one kind of me.

No one can be like me even if they tried

I'm that one star imitated in the dark, night sky.

I am not like every girl you see passing by or on the street, mentally, physically, and definitely

spiritually.

I don't wear makeup, I embrace natural beauty

makeup doesn't define beauty, yes I'm still a cutie.

I like my rosy cheeks, shaded eyelids, and chocolate skin, I am so beautiful that even if I had a twin, I would still win.

Not being arrogant, I just love myself

**If I become a poet, you will find me on your bookshelf.**

No one can think the way I think and feel the way I feel,

my heart has been through so much at a young age it's ridiculous, but as I get older, watch it heal.

This poem was random, this isn't how I usually write, for I write about deeper things that you can't see with your natural eyesight, I have something called foresight.
If you think you know me just cuz' you read this freestyle, baby don't be fooled, you have no idea what's behind this smile.
— 14-year-old Ramyiah's poem

He knows me, knows my soul.

We are from the same star.

We are of the same essence.

When we part from one another at day's break, he says "see you in the stars."

We spend time together in the spiritual realm.

I know him, I know his soul.

We are from the same star.

We are of the same essence.

Texting, we rarely do.

Telepathy, we frequently do.

Telepathy is our spiritual technology,

our means of communication.

He smiles at me with his eyes.

I smile at him with my heart.

He knows me, he knows my soul.

We are from the same star.

We are of the same essence.

my soulmate.

my twin star.

my husband.

— we are one ♡

It took isolation. immense pain and suffering. loving myself deeper and saying no to what I knew wasn't good for me, even if I didn't want to say "no."

self-embrace.

crying on my knees to the Creator for many nights and days.

self-acceptance.

surviving loneliness and depression.

yelling in an empty house for release.

fasting.

watching lectures and sermons.

aching hand, writing for hours at a time.

enduring heavy trials.

losing my mind.

maintaining my sanity.

experiencing a variety of lifestyles.

learning from past experiences.

losing some people along the way.

realizing that nobody will love me,

care for me,

As much as myself and Allah will.

I have no need to look outside of myself for love when love already lives here.

But I can't pretend like I don't want it from the outside world, sometimes.

– bitter sweet truth

It took a lot more than what I've named.

Being molded by my Creator has been so painful, yet so pleasant.

He twists me this way,

bends me that way,

stretches me,

expands me,

in directions that I've shied away from

from the heavens to the depths of the earth,

experiencing moments of pleasure, joy, warmth...

sometimes feeling emotions I have no name for

experiencing a feeling of boredom, staleness

experiencing pain, anger, frustration, sadness

Itching to know what's next when I am asked to be still

This is the process of being molded,

Being fashioned into the work of art He envisioned you and me becoming in the very beginning.

– unique journey

One day, there was an unwavering demand to come to a halt in my life.

 I couldn't help but think about all of the areas in my life where I haven't been living in accord with my nature, which is in direct alignment with Allah's way.

Allah ordered my thoughts in such a way that forced me to come out of confusion, come out of doubt, and come out of the process of denaturing myself.

The continuation of knowingly disobeying God is a heavy pressure that will weigh on us until we are forced to submit by Allah Himself.

If you are straddling the fence between Allah's way and your own way, strive to choose Allah's way every time.

Allah is God and God alone.

Allah is our Father, and we must come to Him with the mind of a child so that He can mold and shape us into what He has willed us to become.

—Matthew 18:3

If only we love deeper and operate from the knowledge that our decisions, thoughts, and habits directly affect those coming after us, we would be more intentional about the way we move and the way we think.

An egocentric person cares not about those coming after them.

To be careless with our progeny is a futile act.

—make a decision

No song is better than a sincere prayer to God.

Not even my "favorite" songs can do for me what conversing with Allah does for me.

They may bring pleasure but only for a moment.

Perhaps we weren't meant to find pleasure in things more than we find pleasure in

praising Him.

So, there's always a yearning for more unless we go to the Source, which is God, for our sustenance.

Music is revolutionary, beautiful, and life-changing.

Music can heal and has healed.

Music is heard on the radio.

We know about that music.

What about the music outside?

Music is heard in nature.

The birds chirping.

The trees swaying.

The tempo of your walk.

The sound of raindrops falling.

Music is a gift from God to us.

Music is medicine to the soul, but it is not the keeper of the soul.

–look for Him in everything

He left her with a heart full of feelings and a mind full of confusion.

injected her with his fluid words.

his appealing vibe.

his intellect.

But he wasn't ready to carry the responsibility of what he had put in her to grow.

Time went on.

The winds began to blow.

The fire began to burn.

She became too much for him.

Why did he awaken her love without the thought of what would come with her love?

Without the thought of responsibility?

I guess that's the risk they took.

That was her last chapter of <u>falling in love with potential.</u>

No more daydreaming of what *could* be. Come to her correct, or don't come at all.

Heartache and frustration will not live here any longer.

Delicate flower, don't ever allow anyone to cause your petals to fall,

your roots to suffer,

 and your leaves to shrivel up.

Grow.

Water yourself.

Sun yourself.

And just like the plant that grows in an upward direction towards the sun

Allow your entire being to grow in an upward direction toward God.

Grow as God intended for you to grow.

Your pain is valid, but you cannot stay here.

Take His hand, and work on being who you deserve to be.

A man worthy of you will come through God to have you,

And your heart won't have to question his presence.

You will know.

– a delicate flower with thorns

My heart was holding on, resisting the ebb and flow of what should be.

You can rest, heart.

Release your stronghold.

Release your grasp.

If you have to hold on so tightly...

So much so that you are straining yourself to keep it...

Then let go.

I give you permission to rest.

I give you permission to be soft, again.

Give your voice meaning again by making your word bond to yourself.

–prioritize showing up for yourself

When coming into knowledge, we come into a big responsibility.

Whatever we know, we will be held responsible for what we do with it.

Perhaps, this is why people choose to stay ignorant.

Ignorance is easygoing, but it's not liberating.

Knowledge is freeing.

To have knowledge of the nature beneath my feet and all around me is liberation.

While I am forging through nature, I find peace in identifying plant species.

To break through language barriers between groups of people is freedom.

When we understand "big words" and languages other than the ones we speak, there's freedom.


To have the knowledge of who and what we are is liberation at its finest.

Our experiences in life have depended and will depend on what we know of ourselves

and how we go about life with what we know.


Knowledge of a complex creature such as a human being is a journey in itself.

There are pages to turn, layers to pull back, moments —and even days—of reflection.

Knowledge of self is so crucial in our development and understanding of the world around us.
After we know who we are, we must have the courage to be who we are, in a world that is always
trying to make us other than our unique selves.

let's take our fingers out of our ears,

remove the blindfold from our eyes,

and separate the lips that have been stitched together, hiding the voice, a beautiful, God-given
instrument, so that someone in the world can receive their blessing.
Liberation comes with a price.

– Are we willing to pay it?

Maybe it was never about getting the degree but about growing my faith to a level that maybe only this circumstance could have done for me in a short time span.

Allah has been building me for what is ahead of me, but I had no idea.

I appeared to be torn down by my experiences.. but on the inside, He was mining me out.

I had been buried so deep in trauma, betrayal, depression, loneliness, guilt, shame...

He said, "Everything must go."

He was making room for who He had in mind for me to be, and I had to be willing to release my hold on all that I believed to be true.

– reflective pause of a muslimah in college

When Islam and I met, it was love at first sight.

–I was born for Islam

O' heart that envies,

 If we can only see in others what is in ourselves,

why is it that your heart can't rejoice at seeing the beauty in someone else?

The truth is that you have the ability to acknowledge the beauty in someone else and so that

means that there is beauty within yourself.

You were one step closer to recognizing your own beauty, but you were interrupted by

ingratitude, and darkness made a home out of your heart.

Heart space full of negativity, spite, and hatred, but it is only for yourself.

Envy stems from a lack of gratitude for what you've already been blessed with.

Gratitude is medicine for the soul, and your heart is in dire need of you to recognize your blessings.

When you've spent a great deal of your life being a people pleaser,

you may also spend a lot of time recovering.

It sounds like me saying "no" when I truly mean "no."

A full-body "no" to remind myself that this is my life,

 and I don't have any business fighting over it with anyone.

It has looked like me honoring who I am at my core and trusting that this is good for me.

Talk about *scary*.

Being your authentic self in a world full of mimicry can be daunting,

*but still,*

You are rewarded with all of the blessings attached to the beautiful person you are.

 Every time I exercise my freedom,

I feel my life force being poured back into me

All of the energy I gave, putting myself in a deficit

All of the energy I gave without true willingness.

Your process of recovery may bewilder those around you.

Don't allow the misunderstanding of others to box you in.

Spread your wings and soar.

That is your birthright.

- beautiful butterfly

You'd be amazed at the difference you make in others just by being your most authentic, beautiful self.

What is the authentic version of you?

The way in which we live and behave authentically, looks different for each of us.

Authenticity is so misunderstood.

Why is authenticity confined to one way of being, when really it is expressed in several different ways?
Is my authenticity invalid just because it isn't like someone else's? No. It is not.

My authenticity is valid, and so is yours.

Our ways of being authentic are different.

Now that I honor that, it's unlikely for me to internalize shade painted with good intentions,
Unlikely for me to allow myself to entertain the notion that the way authenticity looks on me isn't true authenticity.

I am who God made me to be, and though I will continue to evolve, I'm going to cherish the little girl that I am right now.

With myself, I will never have to wait to be loved on.

With Allah, I will never have to wait to be loved on.

It's automatic, and I love that for me.

He loves me and always will.

He confirms that I am on the right path, and always does.

He warns me with gentle reminders.

From self and Allah is all the confirmation I need.

The sweet serenade of victory sounds like yellow & pink in my ears.

She looks up at the sky which appears as a swirl of colors, mixed with intention and precision.

"Allah painted this one," she said.

"He's the Best Artist," he responded.

The soul of Roberta.

My mother has grit,

A woman with a strong personality.

A relentless soul.

Her spirit won't give in.

A giver at heart, she's a selfless woman.

The backbone of our family.

In her ways, she has taught me to never settle for less than I deserve,

to never let up when your worth is high but the offer is low.

to be willing to walk away and know that better is coming,

As. If. You. Got it. Like. That.

And that, I do.

Thank you, mother.

— an angel in disguise

I pray that whoever is being tried in this time persists in goodness and never grows weary in doing good.

When times get hard, apply grace but also apply pressure.

Get to know how much of each you need and when you need it.
*You have time to get to know you.*

There's nothing more important than creating harmony between yourself and God.

There is no higher form of intimacy than the intimacy you cultivate with yourself and God.

So, you *have time* today.

— in the mood to love me

o u t r o

I pray you've received nourishment from this book.

I pray you've received clarity from this book.

I pray you've received divine guidance from this book.

You have witnessed some of the thoughts I have thought, words I have spoken, and feelings I have felt, that have served as catalysts for change in my life. I thank Allah for allowing me to be vulnerable enough to share my experiences with the world, and I am immensely grateful for each soul who has taken the time to read this book.

As a writer, I feel that it is only right that I give you all something to write about. On the next few pages, you will be blessed with journal prompts that have helped me to dig deep into who I am, think in a positive direction, gain nearness to God, and overall, grow. You can also revisit any questions that may have resonated with you from chapters 1 and 2.

You have the freedom to write on a separate piece of paper, a designated journal, or even the space below each journal prompt. If you happen to be somewhere that is peaceful for you, like a nature park or a coffee shop, write to these journal prompts. Even if you are in an environment that isn't inspiring, I encourage you to ask yourself these questions to set a positive atmosphere for yourself. Your mind is powerful, and though your environment may not be all that you want it to be right now, you have the ability to make your *immediate* environment (which is yourself) a good place to be in. Worry not about what you cannot control, and focus your attention on what you can control. Whenever you are ready, you can begin journaling. If ever you feel worried while going deep with yourself, take a break, ask God for His assistance, and do whatever else you need to do to continue to explore the depths of who you are. Take it slow and know that you have time. This is a safe space just for you.

♡

What does your heart yearn for?
Is it a place, a lifestyle, a person, an era, a connection,  material possessions,  a way of being ?
Whatever your heart is yearning for, take time and write it here. Utilize this time to hold space for
yourself. You are safe to express from the depths of your heart, soul, mind, and spirit.

What narratives do I tell myself consistently? When do pieces of those narratives present themselves to me? In what ways do they present themselves to me?

How do I perceive others' views of me? How do I perceive myself? (In other words, what do I think others are thinking about me? How do I think they see me? How do I see myself?)

Do you like the sound of your voice? Does your voice hold weight for you when you hear yourself speak? Does it have meaning for you? If not, why is that so?

When you tell yourself you're going to do something, do you keep your word
to yourself? to others? If not, what are little ways you can begin keeping your
word to yourself and/or others?

What does it mean to be beautiful or attractive to me? Where did I get this meaning from? Do I fit my definition of beautiful or attractive? (Helpful follow-up question: Is your meaning of beauty your own?)

What makes me feel like my best self?
( I want you to think about the things you've done when you felt your
happiest. You may have had times when you have felt very proud of
yourself or confident in who you are. What were you doing in those
moments? What was going on? What was your environment like?)

What do you love about yourself? What do you wish to improve? Who do you need to be to align with the blessings you want?  What about yourself are you willing to work on to acquire and keep your blessings?